# Heal My Broken Pieces

---

TeShanna Rayner

HEAL MY BROKEN PIECES

Copyright © 2019 by TeShanna Rayner

A Racq Symphony Publication

All rights reserved. No part of this book may be reproduced or transmitted in any form or by any means without written permission from the author.

ISBN-13: 978-0-9986627-2-5

ISBN-10: 0-9986627-2-0

*This work is dedicated in memory of my mother, Sammie Rayner.*

*May her legacy of love live on through me.*

*Special dedication to my two heartbeats, Princess Kaleah and Prince Joshua. Thank you for always motivating me towards better.*

# The Journey

Acknowledgements ..................................................................... i

Foreword ................................................................................ iii

The Beginning of Forever........................................................ 1

Mile 0: How Did I Get Here? .................................................. 5

Mile 1: Looking Beyond the Surface ..................................... 9

Mile 2: Identity ...................................................................... 15

Mile 3: These Roots Run Deep.............................................. 19

Mile 4: Bad Roots Yield Bad Fruit........................................ 23

Mile 5: Bondage vs. Boundaries .......................................... 31

Mile 6: Journey to Wholeness.............................................. 33

Mile 7: The Process of Love.................................................. 37

Mile 8: Newness .................................................................... 41

Mile 9: Recalibrate & Recondition...................................... 45

The Never-Ending Mile: Maintaining Your Wholeness........... 49

My Road Trip Called Life ..................................................... 55

Daily Affirmations................................................................ 61

Inner Healing & Emotional Wholeness Prayer ................. 63

Emotional Healing Scriptures ............................................. 65

## Acknowledgements

I am most grateful to God for allowing me to go through all that I have, with a victorious triumph over all of my obstacles and through all of my experiences, mistakes, and wrong decisions. I appreciate Him for allowing me to share my journey with others and to be inspiration and testament of the saving and healing power of Jesus Christ.

I would like to say a special thank you to the people who influenced this book... who I've encountered at different times in my life...who caused me to mature and understand my process of healing to wholeness. I appreciate the experiences and the lessons.

I would like to thank my family and friends who all inspired me through this writing process. Special shout out to my daddy, John aka "Big Poppa", Grandma Barbara, my late grandparents, John and Buelah Sutton, "Godma" Eleanor, Goddaddy "Zeke", Auntie Rosa Mae, and my siblings (by blood and love): Shelly, Michael, Dawn, Shawn, Cindy, Dot, Lisa, Mia, Sabrina, Kristina, Renae, Johnae, Teia, Courtney, AJ, and Chris...my girls: Shakita, Yolanda, Shae, Nicci, Shadira, Amber, Elouise, Cici, Keshia, Bridgette, Ashley, Everlena, Tiana, Precious, Kennetha, Stephanie, and Capree- y'all have been my support though some really rough times. I love y'all to life!

I would like to say a special thank you to my best friend, Shakita Dixon, for riding on this journey from brokenness to healing to wholeness with me. You have seen every broken piece and helped me to allow God to put me back together again. Thank you for pushing me to do this book and for going before me with your writings and helping me piece everything together. Thank you for pushing me out of my comfort zone and into my purpose zone. You're more of a sister than blood could ever make us. I love you to life! #myRacq

I would like to say a special thanks to Dr. Mark Jones, my pastor, for pushing me and helping me to grow to the place where I can be unapologetically myself and accomplish this writing because it was what God purposed me to do. I would like to thank Prophetess Michelle Guess, Pastor Shilita Ferguson, Pastor Tish Bryant, and Lady Tamieka "First" Gaines for mentoring me, holding me accountable, and pushing me out of my comfort zone and pulling purpose out of me.

To Kimberly Hemmingway - my teacher, my coach, my friend (and sometimes my mirror) - thank you for pushing me out of the box, helping me to focus, and empowering me to make a God-sized dent in this world. Your wisdom is priceless: *"...nothing but greatness...always checked in!"*

Lastly, a special thank you goes to all of my pastors & spiritual leaders who invested wisdom, correction, and love to raise me up from a little girl to a strong woman of faith: Bishop James E. Byrd & the late Mother Isabelle Byrd, Bishop-Elect S. Lamar Simmons, the late Lady Telephia Jackson, Elder Ansen Goyens, Pastor Oliver King & Lady Colette King, and Apostle Mark T. Jones & Lady Lisa Jones. The guidance, counsel, wisdom, and spiritual knowledge that you have poured into me is priceless. I will cherish you all eternally!

# Foreword

Wholeness comes in pieces. Our God loves and cares for us and is always working a plan to bring us to "expected ends" as Jeremiah 29:11 says. It is discerning and allowing the process that can be the greatest challenge. In this publication, *Heal My Broken Pieces*, author, TeShanna Rayner, will encourage you on your journey to wholeness, one piece at a time.

*Dr. Mark T. Jones*
*Manifestations Worldwide Inc.*

## The Beginning of Forever

"It is so hard to deal with the fact that I made decision after decision that didn't meet up to most people's expectations of me...to my expectations of me...and God's. I can't call this a mistake...sure at first, it was. I let my guard down. But, after a while, a repeated intentional mistake looks a lot like (and is) an intentional choice. Wow! I lowered my standards because I didn't love myself enough not to...too busy trying to pour love into people who didn't love me back with the same intensity...trying to fill their voids, which was supposed to be reciprocated and equate to somehow filling mine. That's hard to deal with because you would think I would know better enough to do better...but I was stuck on stupid... doing dumb stuff over and over again...getting deeper and deeper into my mess...and that makes me feel like damaged goods (with stains, rips, and discoloration and irregularities) not good enough for anybody to even want to love because of my indiscretions. I feel so empty and broken. My life is in pieces...scattered pieces. I'm so overwhelmed with emotion right now...I can't even put it all into words...my tears are speaking what my heart feels. Lord, please heal my broken pieces..."

Reflecting now at this journal entry I wrote some years back, I was in a place of despair and in desperate need of repair. My heart was hurting. And, to tell you the truth, the pain did not happen overnight. It did not occur with one season of bad decision-making or one bad relationship. However, the pain revealed how relationally challenged I was, not only with potential life mates but with others I cared about, and most importantly with God. I was engaging people, life, and God from a fragmented perspective and a broken place. I remember that "heal my broken pieces" prayer like it was yesterday. While so simple, those words were my huge cry to God to take the wheel and drive me far away from that place. I was tired of the cycle, and I wanted to— no needed to— feel whole and live whole. Just as the damage and pain had not occurred over night, a span of time was necessary to heal into my whole self again.

As you read *Heal My Broken Pieces*, please understand that your process of brokenness to wholeness is a journey. This composition was birthed through my thoughts, emotions, prayers, reflection, insights, and the Divine encouragement I experienced during my journey to becoming a whole person. While some aspects may be written for women from a woman's perspective, it is definitely meant to help any broken person. This book will serve as a roadmap to help guide your journey.

As with traveling to any destination, there may be several routes you can take to arrive at a single location. As a matter of fact, some routes take longer than others. Inclement weather, traffic delays, accidents, road construction, vehicle mechanical issues, and necessary pit stops all affect the time and manner in which you arrive to your intended destination. Usually, through our life's experiences, we tend to take the scenic route full of detours that provide lessons from which we grow. However, I want to challenge you to be expedient about getting to this place of wholeness in your life. Yes, it will take some time, but how you govern yourself on the journey will determine how long and how smooth the ride will be. The sooner you can get there, the sooner you will begin to experience an abundance of contentment, joy, peace, and richness in your life and your relationships with others. I will be your chauffeur and your travel mate, so feel free to take this road trip with me...buckle up...let's go...

Welcome to the journey! This is the beginning of forever...

**Mile 0: How Did I Get Here?**

Mile zero designates the starting point of the journey. While our backgrounds, experiences, and routes may all be different, with varying miles traveled to our now place, we all started somewhere, at some place and moment in time. However, to understand the process of our journey, we must understand not only where we started, but how we arrived to our current place and state of brokenness. Sometimes we have to back trace our steps in order to find out the starting point of the route we took that ended to a destination of brokenness and dysfunction. It is also important when analyzing the where and how, to also think back to the road signs and traffic lights we dismissed or did not pay attention to at all. I once wrote a Facebook status that was a reminder and wakeup call for myself and my followers: How many signs must one see to realize you are driving down a dead-end road? #turnaround #chooseanotherroute. The signs and the signals are there for our safety and protection to ensure the most favorable road experience.

Likewise, often times we end up broken because we are not protected. We open ourselves up and are vulnerable to people instead of being vulnerable to God. We take Him out of the front seat of our heart. As a result, instead of allowing His omniscience to lead us, we end up governing ourselves, while God takes a backseat to our feelings and emotions. And, normally, we end up settling for less than God's best because He has not directed us. While it is easy to allow our emotions and even our intellect and knowledge to pave the road of our decision-making, we must passionately pursue God's best for our lives. In order to do that we must start with a thorough examination of the driver of the car we are in: SELF.

Take a moment to look at yourself in the mirror...not a hand-held compact mirror, not the rearview mirror nor the pull-down mirror in the sun visor, but a full body mirror that shows a reflection of who you are. While standing in front of that mirror, we have to look beyond the reflection and in that intangible space—the place that you can see with your eyes closed. We are comprised of more than the skin, bones, and organs that complete our body. We are made up of our minds, our heart, our soul, our spirit, and our emotions. But, when we yield to the Spirit of God and allow Him to take over and allow Him control of our emotions sincerely, then we are better suited to make decisions that are closely aligned to what He wants for our life. I know it sounds strange because we always hear that we are the "captain of our ship is and the master of our fate", and yes to a certain extent we can be all of the above, but when we allow God to be in control of that, then our whole person becomes more beautiful because we allowed Him to breathe on us and to touch our entire being (body, mind, spirit, and emotions). We cannot continue to take this journey based on how we feel because feelings are fickle. Our feelings change depending on the circumstance, based on chemical and/or hormonal imbalance, and all types of influences in our lives. So, we cannot move off of how we feel, but we must make sound decisions… especially when it comes to relating to people.

    The Bible says that if we delight ourselves (meaning find enjoyment and contentment) in God, He will give us the desires of our heart (Psalm 37:4) and that He will perfect the thing concerning us or, in other words, fulfill His purpose and plan for our lives (Psalm 138:8). However, how is it possible and how can we rightly expect for Him to give us the desires of our hearts that are not aligned to His will? It is because He is not seated on the throne seat of our heart. When we put God first, when we make Him first, when we make His purpose and His will for our lives a priority, we no longer have to worry about having desires that are not fitted to His will and agenda for us because He begins to snuff out, smoke out, take out, and burn out those things that are detrimental to us. Yes, it's a process. No, it won't happen overnight.

## Mile 1: Looking Beyond the Surface

Are you the person that when you meet a potential mate and you find him or her attractive and the feelings seem mutual or at the very least he or she shows some type of interest, you have already planned your wedding, given your unborn children their names, and pictured a life-long time together? Are you the type of woman or man that when you meet somebody and they show genuine interest in you, you are so closed and bottled up in fear of being hurt again that you don't give anybody a chance or allow them to be close enough to get to know the real you? Are you the type of woman that gives everybody a chance with no intention to commit to anyone at any level, trying to think like a man and convince yourself that if you trust no one then nobody can take advantage of you? These are dysfunctional thoughts and behaviors that lead to a cycle and eventually an acceptable normalcy of dysfunction that is not God's best nor His intended purpose for us and our relationships with men and women. However, the only way to stop a cycle is to put something counter active in its track.

One necessary step we must take to change our direction of thought, is to become transparent while looking in the mirror at self. Not only must we become transparent, but we have to be vulnerable enough to allow this examination to expose all of the things inside of us that have been covered up but not cured. We have to strip before God — allow Him to strip us — and touch those hurting places that are hidden. Allow Him to touch those injured, damaged places. When there is an infection to any area of your body and cleansing and healing does not occur, it slowly deteriorates. It begins to get gangrene; it rots; and it becomes infectious to the other healthy parts in your body. If you do not amputate, extract, and cut out the decaying and rotten areas within, the other productive areas of your life suffer: your professional life; your health; your mental state; how you relate to people on your job; how you relate to your children; how you interact with your spouse; how you relate to your family and friends; etc. You will start to see life and filter situations and occurrences through the lens of a dying or dead perspective. That is certainly not God's best for you.

    Know that He wants you to have His very best that He has intended for your life, but you have to allow yourself to be open so that He can see what is inside and assess what is broken and needs to be fixed. Take a package, for instance, that has been nicely sealed up. There is an expensive present inside. It has been gift wrapped, and now it is being shipped to its destination. But, along the way to its destination it was picked up and dropped. It was kicked around. Its cargo truck was in a few accidents along the way, and so it was tossed around and the gift inside became shattered and broken. It can be repaired or replaced, and the thought of the gift itself has not lost its value. The gift may be damaged right now, but once it is replaced, it is more valuable. How is that possible? It now costs more when we consider its original cost, plus the repair or replacement costs, in addition to the insurance costs, and the labor costs for the time and effort of repairing or rebuilding what was inside of the box. However, in order to assess the damage that has been done — in order to see what is broken and what needs to be repaired or even replaced — it has to be opened up. The outer packaging has to be cut off, torn off, or ripped off in order to open the box and see the contents inside. That gift that we have inside of us — our love, trust, commitment, and all of the unique characteristics the Creator has placed within the fiber of our being and the fabric of who we are individually— and what we have to offer somebody else has to be opened up. And, who better to open us up than the One who created us and put the gifts inside the box. The

Person who gifted and shipped the gift off to the destination was not responsible for the damage that was done, but He takes ownership for assessing the damage and the value of the gift so that it can be replaced.

There are some things that God wants to completely remove out of the fiber of who we are because it is a generational curse, passed down in our emotional DNA, through decisions that our parents and grandparents and their parents and grandparents made. So, if the history of the family is characterized by being a womanizer or a whore, or being abusive in any way, or being deceitful, dishonest, and disloyal, then God wants to take those traits out of you. This is why it is so vital for us, as the driver on our journey, to allow God to open us up and see every part of our damaged selves and be real, transparent, and not in denial of those things that abhor us...those things that disappoint us... those areas where we are flawed... those areas where we are wrong in our hearts. We have a skewed perspective and are relationally dysfunctional when we are looking at life and viewing things out of damaged lenses. We do not want to be or remain that way, so we have to pray, "Lord, heal my broken pieces! Heal the damaged areas of my heart and soul. I am opening up to You so that You can assess the value of the damage that has been done, and so that You know how to fix it and how to replace it."

## Mile 2: Identity

Often times, we lose our identities becoming who he, she, and they thought we should be. We pour so much ourselves into them and we are so loyal to them that we become disloyal to our own truths and our own identity. We lose ourselves or we give ourselves away to the things that do not fall back into us. We give ourselves away for free or without any reciprocity or return on our investment because we have lost or minimized our own value to accept the value that other placed on us. One day we may be valuable and the next day, maybe not. In his or her mind we are disposable because they have gotten everything that they wanted. They have achieved their goals, and once they have accomplished that which they set out to do, our value or utility to them has decreased.

This mindset is a roadblock to the journey. Likewise, when this occurs we stop forward movement altogether and withdraw into a mental cave. While in the darkness of the cave, we focus on an identity that has been internally carved and weathered by those hurtful experiences. Thus, caves allow us to hide our brokenness and hinder us from getting the healing and wholeness. Now, there is a difference between a cave and a cocoon. A cocoon is for transformation towards restoration, newness, and wholeness. The cocoon adds value, makes you better, and causes you to become who you were created to be, even if you look another way now. To push through the roadblock and fight through the "cave moments", we must truly learn who we are and distinguish our purpose and value. This only comes through learning our Creator. See, we were made in His likeness and image. Therefore, we have to understand who He is and how He is in order to understand *who* we are supposed to be, *how* we are supposed to be, how we are supposed to *act*, how we are supposed to *think*, and how we are supposed to *see ourselves*. Do we see God as damaged goods? Do we see Him as broken pieces? Do we see Him desolate, in despair, depressed, downtrodden, or a victim? Even when Christ was on the cross, He was not a victim; He was the victor! But, in the transformation process, it is difficult to see that because...it is a process. These things take time.

Just like the caterpillar transforming into the butterfly, there is a process, and each stage in the process has some level of growth to be achieved in order for the next stage to take place. It may sound cliché, but trust the process and do not rush the process! It is just like a baby preparing to be born. It takes a nine-month term. Some babies who are born prematurely face the possibility of higher risk for complications, birth defects, and long-term health issues because these things take time. Every month of the birthing phase is critical to the physical development of the baby, both inside and out. Likewise, there is a level of strength that comes at each growth phase, and even when the baby is born there is another level and a new dimension of growth that must take place. It cannot stay in the infancy stage all of its life, neither can it remain a toddler or an adolescent, but it has to grow to become a productive adult.

This is the same way with our healing journey. Just like the transformation from the caterpillar in the cocoon to become the butterfly or a baby going from an embryo to an infant to a toddler to an adult, we have to allow our healing to go through its phases. There is a level of strength that comes with each phase of our healing. There is growth and development that comes in each phase of our healing. Although healing is not a stagnant process, it is a process, and we cannot rush it because we can stunt out development, arrive prematurely, and have to face the possibility of emotional defects and lasting issues; and as a result, we will tend to identify with being defected and dysfunctional, rather than being whole.

## Mile 3: These Roots Run Deep

*God, You're making me deal with this dark place...this place that I swore I would take to my grave. I've only shared this secret with one person. My family doesn't know. My best friends don't know. But, You want me to tell the world my testimony so I can be forever free?!? You want me to dig up these roots so you can plant new seeds?!? (Sigh) Well, I won't allow fear to grip me any longer...here goes nothing...and everything...at the same time...Lord, heal my broken pieces!*

*Perversion, low self-esteem, fear...I can pinpoint exactly when these seeds were planted in my life. I was 6 years old. I was molested by a teenage friend of the family. I was violated by someone who my mother trusted to care for me. I did not fully understand, but I knew it was neither good nor right. I was afraid to tell my mother or her parents because I didn't want to get her in trouble. I felt trapped and afraid. I just wanted it to stop. Eventually it did, but it left a scar deep within that opened the door for other influences. From that point in my life until now, I can see the effects that moment had in various connections and relationships. I think one of the greatest effects was that it left me vulnerable to putting myself in a position to be hurt and hurt other people. Twenty-seven years later and it still affects me. These roots run deep...*

This part of the journey requires you to slow down, be alert, and pay attention. This is not a place where you can afford to be distracted or set back. Most importantly, do not crash. If you crash at this point, more damage may be caused and more rehabilitation may be necessary in order for you to start your journey over again. Recently, I was in a seemingly minor car accident, rear-ended with dents and damage to the back of my car. After the initial assessments were made on my vehicle, an estimate for the damage was sent to the insurance claims adjuster. However, once the auto repair company began to take apart the outer pieces that were damaged, they found more internal damages that affected other parts and functionality to my car. Although it was only a month, it seemed like forever before I finally got my car back. But, because there was so much underlying damage caused by the crash, the inside pieces of my car had to be fixed before the outside could even be addressed. And that was just the damage to my car, as I am still in the rehabilitation process to be able to walk, dance, clean, sleep, (and anything else that requires me to move) normally and pain-free again. So, please, do not crash, as your journey to healing may be severely delayed.

Likewise, at this juncture, you must understand that it doesn't matter how mistreated, mishandled, used, abused, damaged, or broken you are; God can heal you and make you whole. Free yourself from the hurt and connect to the Healer! But, in order to be free, you must identify the root of the matter...the hidden, suppressed, and buried issues that fertilize your hurt and keep you in cycles of brokenness and dysfunction. If you don't deal with buried issues from "peopleships" and "situationships" you will never be able to have a healthy relationship with anyone. Molestation... rape...physical abuse... verbal abuse... being cheated on, lied to, or used...loss of a loved one...cycles of dysfunction...these are many of the issues that build the history and testimony of our experiences. Our experiences have been like seeds planted in our life. Over time, these seeds become buried and suppressed under our everyday routine and guise of normal functionality. However, the longer we ignore or try to forget these seeds were planted, and failure to address our issues in a healthy way, only waters and nurtures them. Then, the seeds grow roots and ultimately produce fruit. These fruits are spiritual manifestations of demonic attack against our soul and become a mask over our true identity.

As with a house, roots that are untamed and unattended can cause damage and cracking to your emotional and mental foundation. Thus, dealing with roots require you to look beyond the reflection in the mirror and to look deep within and recall experiences, incidents, words spoken, acts committed, and feelings evoked that fractured and hammered away at your soul. While everyone's journey is different, there are some common issues that need to be addressed and rooted out of our souls so that we do not produce and yield bad fruit.

## Mile 4: Bad Roots Yield Bad Fruit

Insecurity

Let's talk about insecurities. How exactly does one get over insecurities? I believe it starts with and is magnified as a result of trust issues. In my opinion, our trust issues with people reflect of lack of trust in God. To be transparent, one of the hardest things about being a natural born leader and administrator is stepping back, taking my hands off the control panel, and trusting that God will land me in the right place, with the right people, at the right time. I used to be a bit of a control freak, and I have to conscientiously remind myself that I cannot control other people (what they do, how they feel, what they think or perceive, etc.), nor can I be in control of every aspect of my life. If that were the case, I would not need to rely on God. Proverbs 3:5-6 (AMP) says, "Trust in and rely confidently on the Lord with all your heart, and do not rely on your own insight or understanding. In all your ways know and acknowledge and recognize Him, and He will make your paths straight and smooth [removing obstacles that block your way]". When you trust in God and remain confident in the purpose and value that He placed within you, there is a power and a peace that neither outside forces nor other people can take away.

To be insecure means that one is either not sure or not safe. When you are not safe or you feel unsure, you have to examine yourself first. Sometimes you have to look at negative things that were said, perceptions of others that was impressed upon you, and your own self-perception. If you do not deal with insecurities, you allow room for the enemy to play with your mind. It is no one else's responsibility to manage your insecurities or your liberation from the anxiety that comes with it. You must do the work of leaning into the strength and peace of God and releasing the need to control what is outside of you.

Likewise, it is imperative, I mean highly important for you to understand the difference between insecurities versus your God-given discernment. I am not telling you to neglect intuition and discernment, but make sure it comes from a healthy place and not derived based upon negative experiences that have altered your mindset and caused the lack of trust. You have to learn to let go of insecurities and mistrust and ask God to give you discernment...sharp, strong, confident discernment which requires constant, unblocked conversation and intimacy with Him. If you do not rid yourself of those mind toxins, you will always be skeptical of the intensions, motives, and love displayed by others. It is okay and sometimes wise to be guarded or cautious, but stop making comparisons and expecting to receive the same bad treatment as your past situations and experiences. Put the umbrella and rain shoes away; stop looking for the rain when the sun is shining and the sky is clear. Wipe off the lens of your relational eyes, and view each interaction as a fresh encounter. And, if you find patterns or trends of characteristics in the people you encounter and connect with, then pullover, pull down the visor, open the mirror, and take a good look at yourself. You may need to back up to Mile 1 or 2 before moving ahead.

## Loneliness

In your time of loneliness and desperation do not allow the enemy to influence you to do unconventional things that are normally outside of your character. These are the things that seem right but are detrimental to your reputation, character, integrity, and destiny. These are things that you will later regret and eventually find yourself feeling guilty over or like you owe everybody an explanation. The enemy of your soul will use and magnify those situations — times of loneliness and times of yearning, longing, desiring of a void to be filled — against you. He will send the wrong somebody to come along and show you attention that is substance-less, surface, and not fulfilling. But, because you are filtering your connection through the root of being lonely, it appears to be just what you desire and need, and they make a connection with you hooking into that root. That relationship or connection or attention is magnified and will have you believing that it is something and something special and significant, when it is really nothing more than a mechanism to fracture your heart and soul again. A truly whole person would not have a root of loneliness for someone to hook into but rather a solid foundation of contentment to build upon.

Lust

When you are operating out of lust you make stupid decisions because your judgement is clouded by fleshly desires. 1 Peter 4:8 says that "love covers a multitude of sins." The spirit of lust seeks to expose your weaknesses and covers nothing; there may be a temporary cover up, but the after effects can be detrimental because consistent yielding to lust will gravitate toward a demise. Lust tries to disguise itself as love, but it plays on your emotions and your soulish realm and becomes the dominant spirit that leads you. Lust is not just sexual. It has other characteristics that all lead to perversion: appropriating, using, handling, the right things/people the wrong way or other than its original or intended purpose and use.

Manipulation

Manipulation is a form of witchcraft. It seeks amplified control of actions, emotions, thoughts, and opinions through guilt, lies, and intimidation. Manipulation preys on weaknesses, vulnerabilities, and low self-esteem. Through observation and experience, I have found that manipulative people have often suffered from being manipulated by others, and instead of healing from the pain of the experience, manipulation becomes a coping mechanism. In your journey to becoming whole, you must be careful not to replicate this behavior. You cannot become better by making others feels worse. Failure to cut off manipulative tendencies will result in a reciprocation of the same treatment.

Entitlement

The spirit of entitlement breeds manipulation and causes you to become even more broken than you started out to be. You have to understand that your healing process is just that — yours! Nobody owes you anything, but you owe it to yourself and to your purpose and your destiny to become whole. Whether somebody apologizes or not, you forgive. Whether somebody gives you recompense or not, pay yourself back with the opportunity to become a whole person. Never let anybody control your emotions to the point where you become bitter because once bitterness spreads it is hard to get it out of your system. You do not want to heal with bitterness in your heart because that is like having an infection underneath a wound that is healing. When you have an infection on the inside of something that is healing it becomes gangrenous and like a cancer, and then it has to be cut off. You do not want to have to have any part of your purpose, your destiny, or your character cut off because you allow the genuine thing to become rotten.

Resentment

Resentment is a cocktail mixed with unforgiveness, bitterness, anger, and disappointment. This bad fruit is rooted in painful experiences of having unmet or unfulfilled expectations or being hurt repeatedly, seemingly with no regard. Resentment is most often internalized and takes an emotional and mental toll on the person harboring resentment, sometimes unbeknownst to the other person. It acts like a silent killer of a slow death. Imagine being stabbed in the heart over and over, and screaming loudly, but the sound only being heard in your mind, muted to the outside world. That is what resentment does. It imprisons the mind and confines us to a place of fear and expectations of being let down. Ephesians 4:31 encourages us to rid ourselves of bitterness and forgive. If resentment is not released and forgiveness is not forged, this fruit will further rot into hatred and spite. I have read before that resentment and unforgiveness is like drinking poison and expecting the other person to die. The resentment cocktail only leads to rotten, dead places in the soul that causes cracking and ultimately broken fragments of the heart.

## Mile 5: Bondage vs. Boundaries

Chains have a multipurpose. They are used to protect and guard and to keep something bound. Sometimes in our relationships and interactions with people, what is meant for protection and what is meant as a safeguard becomes bondage and a hindrance to our destiny. For instance, if someone purchases a storage and they put a chain and a lock on the storage, it is to safeguard and protect their personal items from theft; however, if the storage agreement and the contract is breached, and that connection is broken for lack of payment or lack of a fulfillment of the contract, then the chain and the lock are illegally there. So, it is no longer a safeguard, but now it is something hindering the occupancy of that space for someone or something else that will be in compliance and agreement with the standards of the contract. Therefore, it is imperative that illegal chains and the things that are keeping us bound be loosened. Sometimes chains are broken. Sometimes chains simply fall off. And, sometimes chains must be cut. Whatever the case, identify the chains in your life. Determine if they are safeguards that promote boundaries or a hindrance that promotes bondage.

Likewise, once God begins to heal you have to make sure that you establish Godly connections and

Godly relationships with boundaries that align to your prophetic destiny and plan for your life. When you see the cancer of an old cycle of bondage trying to rear its head again in a new relationship or a reconstructed/healed relationship, then you have to nip that at the bud so that it does not infiltrate the roots, the stems, the leaves, or the fruit of the new connection. Why? Because bondage hinders your healing and growth. If a new connection or relationship has the power to overtake you and put you back in the same mental, emotional, or spiritual position as before, you have to assess and address it early on so you can continue to walk in healing, deliverance, and in wholeness. Bondage breaks you down and confines you to the place of perpetual brokenness. In contrast, boundaries create a healthy space of freedom that promotes wholeness. When you set your boundaries and communicate the expectation for others to respect your boundaries, it makes it difficult for the bad seeds that fragment your soul and produce bad fruit to be planted into your life.

## Mile 6: Journey to Wholeness

Brokenness attracts brokenness. It is like a magnet; the shards and pieces of one's life seem to fit perfectly with the shards of brokenness in another person's. If you are not whole within yourself and you try to repair a broken relationship, you do not have the solid foundation or wherewithal to build anything with anyone else because that other person will constantly have to work to build you or vice versa. When you are in a broken place, remember that you have to evaluate the root causes for your actions, behaviors, and especially connections. Two broken people do NOT equate a whole. One broken person and a whole person together do NOT equate a whole either. Two whole people need to connect in order for proper function to occur. For instance, consider a broken cup and a broken plate attracting to each other and trying to fit together. The broken pieces although fused together will not be functional because you do not drink from a plate and primarily do not eat from a cup. So, it doesn't matter how much you would put the cup handle on the plate or the bottom or top of a plate on a cup, it will not work, it will not function, and you will be miserable.

When we allow ourselves to mature to wholeness we have to understand that it takes only one experience or decision to break us again. We have to actively and on purpose maintain our wholeness. We have to learn to be okay and content with not receiving less than what we deserve just to say we have. Know your worth. I would rather not have what I deserve than have less than or what I do not deserve. Too many times we accept pieces of others because that is what we are used to giving of ourselves. We give our all so much until we fail to realize we are depleted. It is like driving a luxury vehicle and allowing the gas tank to become empty, but continuing to drive. That vehicle's engine—the vital part necessary for it to function and serve its purpose—is damaged by fumes and garbage from running on E.

Similarly, brokenness leads us to make broken decisions. There is a logical sequence to our thought patterns and our decision-making. Essentially, our decision screen is broken and we are unable to process the "is this right?" or "should I do this?" or "will this decision benefit me?" questions properly. Our judgment becomes skewed because we are broken. Sometimes, we have a perception or false sense of wholeness because we have not allowed the pieces of other people to be removed from our heart and soul. We must release these fragments and broken pieces of others so our decision screen is clear and we can live in the fullness of our Creator.

It is also easy to try to do self-repair by picking up the pieces of our shattered hearts and broken lives. However, the fallacy comes when we try to use the wrong glue to keep ourselves together (sex, pornography, drugs, alcohol, money and materialistic things, other people, etc.). We try to fill the void and fill those crevices and spaces created by brokenness with these things, and all the temporary filling does is numb us and provide a temporary escape from dealing with the root of the issue.

One may say that it is too difficult to deal with the hurt and pain on your own. But, 2 Corinthians 12:9 reminds us that God's strength is perfected in your weakness. Therefore, some issues and hurts cannot be solved with human strength; but total healing and deliverance to wholeness requires a Divine power, a Divine connection, and a reliance on the Divine Being. If God wanted you to deliver yourself, He would have never sacrificed Jesus. If it were meant for you to put yourself back together again, then He would not be the Potter as mentioned in Jeremiah 18. These moments of the shattered place when you are trying to pick up the pieces, lean into the strength and healing power of God. Allow Him to take the fragments, the brokenness, the hurt, pain, frustration, disappointments, weakness, low points, dark past, and gruesome history and put it on His wheel. Allow Him to smooth out the jagged edges into a beautiful, whole, uncracked, untarnished, valuable work of art.

## Mile 7: The Process of Love

When you think of the word process what comes to mind? I think of development, progression, time, investment, and return. The process of love requires investment of your mind, emotions, heart, and soul over time. Likewise, in the process of love, we have to stop falling in love with the idea of love and the potential of love. Sometimes, we have to evaluate love, or what we refer to as love, at face value and not potential worth because we may end up falling in love with a lie or a false reality instead of the development and progression of something pure.

The process of genuine love takes time. However, that process begins with getting to know yourself in order to undo the thought patterns that others placed inside of you, to take off the mask that others gave to you, and to rid yourself of the self-esteem that others *allowed* you to have. As stated earlier, knowing and understanding self requires that you know and understand your Healer and Creator, which reflects His definition of you. Scripture states that you were made in His likeness and image and that you are fearfully and wonderfully made. Therefore, there is nothing inferior about you. There is nothing damaged within you because He did not create you inferior nor damaged, despite your past decisions and experiences.

God is able to and does make all things new. Knowing this, I encourage anyone to never give up on love, but take time to learn love. The Bible says in I John 4: 7-8, "Let us love one another: for love is of God...for God is love." It is impossible to truly love anybody else until you first learn to love yourself, and you cannot fully love yourself until you learn to love the One who made you and grasp an understanding of the depth of His love. My pastor, Dr. Mark T. Jones said, "We look to others to secure or love us, but that is God's job so that we come to any relationship ready to give what we already have." See, God's love is unconditional. Corinthians 13 provides an explicit narrative of love when it states, "Love is patient. Love is kind. Love does not keep a record of wrong-doing..." Often times we think that that love —agape love— should only be achieved from God's standpoint... that only Jesus is supposed to love us like that, but, you are supposed to love like that as well. For instance, you have to love yourself enough to stop record-keeping the wrongdoing that you have done in your life because that is only a guilt trip the enemy sends to try to keep you bound. Yes, you made mistakes! Yes, you did not make the best decisions, but through the process of love, you are healing towards better.

When you desire is to love yourself and others purely and purposefully, healing is necessary. And, the process of God's love will go into the hidden places to ensure true wholeness. God must remove the old skin... the dead skin... the scab that you allowed to be infected by brokenness underneath and touch what is spreading gangrenous in side of you... the thing that infects your heart and mind because you did not allow it to be purified and cleansed properly before it could heal. But, through the process of His love, God is cleansing and removing the things inside of you that will cause you to be stagnant in your healing. He is cleansing the things that infect your mindset. He is allowing a new skin to heal and form. One that is more beautiful than it was before, yet more resistant to the things that used to cause you harm.

**Mile 8: Newness**

New does not always mean better, and better does not always mean new, but when God puts His hands on something, either brand new or renewed, it is the best! In any case, shun not your renewal process, as it could result in the very thing that you asked God for. Isaiah 43:19 reminds us that God has already begun to do something new in our lives. The newness begins in the mind, influences your actions, and takes over your life until you are healed and whole.

God can accelerate your healing with His holy wind. Just as God blew breath in Adam's lungs and life became, God wants to blow on your fragmented pieces and cause them to come together. He wants to heal you of your broken pieces, but you have to allow all the pieces to be there. You have to give Him every piece with no holding back. You must present it all to Him. It does not matter how many pieces, how big, how tiny, or how crushed, give Him all the pieces! Like only He can, as the Master Potter, as the Master Artist, as God our Creator, the Master Creator, He can blow the wind of newness on those pieces and form a new creature…a new you. The Bible says in 2 Corinthians 5:17, "If any man be in Christ, he is a new creature." Allow Christ's wind to revive, refresh, renew, and redeem you.

Likewise, the wind is indicative of a new season in your life. As the seasons change, and winter comes, the leaves that were once vibrant with green life turn colors, wither, and fall to the ground...and sometimes they are even blown away in the wind. The weather changes and requires heavier garments to be worn to cover and protect you from the elements. The winter fruit is harvested and even some new seeds are planted for the next season's crop. The same goes on in your life. When the seasons change, you have to learn to be alright with the things that die and blow out of your life. You must accept the new. I would be remiss if I did not tell you that the newness may not feel good or comfortable initially. However, to transition successfully into newness, you must adapt to the chill of life, guard yourself, and gird yourself so that you can stand through the cold, blizzards, and storms. Moreover, you have to strategically plant seeds and invest in the harvest of the next season before you even see it, while reaping the harvest of now. Change is inevitable, but the way you prepare for and respond to change will determine and set the tone for your change experience. Rest in the newness and accept the peace and power that comes with it.

## Mile 9: Recalibrate & Recondition

It is important to establish a new normal when embracing your newness and walking in wholeness. Two key aspects needed to accomplish that new normal is recalibration and reconditioning. Employing the combination of these two dynamics is like pressing a reset button from your past and into your future. To understand how to properly recalibrate and recondition our lives, we must first understand the definition of calibrate and condition as it relates to our inner healing and wholeness process. As noted by dictionary.com, the meaning for calibrate stated to "correct a situation or make something right", while another example of the word recalibrate, according to Cambridge English Dictionary, indicated "to change the way you do or think about something." Likewise, dictionary.com specified the meaning of condition was "to put in a proper state or to accustom or inure" (or to season, toughen, or temper). Equally, recondition means "to restore to a good or satisfactory condition, repair, or make over." In our broken, shattered state we usually become accustomed to *(condition)* and make it right to *(calibrate)* accept that which is subpar and below our standards. However, in your healing process the cornerstone for your foundation of wholeness is to recalibrate and recondition your mind and emotions to truly experience your new normal of healing and wholeness.

I can remember in high school as a cheerleader, before the regular season started, we went through lots conditioning. We performed several exercises, weightlifted, and pushed our bodies to increase our endurance and stamina during games and competitions. That is the same mentality that I take now for my emotional and relational wellbeing. Daily, I have to recalibrate and recondition my mindset, body, emotions, attitude, perception, and expectations in order to have the necessary strength and resilience in my interactions, connections, and relationships with others. I know this may sound strange, but for all of the psychological aerobics we performed from being on emotional rollercoasters in situationships, and for all of the mental weightlifting we did by accepting foolishness and treatment that devalued our self-worth, we must push ourselves even more to maintain our wholeness. That may look like saying positive affirmations to ourselves or blocking and deleting people out of our phone and off our social media. It also means being assertive in letting people know they you are not accepting anything less than

God's best for you. I am in no way suggesting for you to act elite or like you are better than anyone but your old self; however, I am encouraging you to end the cycle of passively enabling others to break you or keep you stuck in old, dysfunctional patterns and out of your newness.

Moreover, as with physical exercise, where the body is transformed and made over, this emotional and inner healing workout will transform the broken pieces of your past (and/or present) into your new normal. And, if you have any question about what your new normal looks like, allow me to paint the picture; it is: valuing your identity, worth, and uniqueness, while rejecting anything less than God's best for you. It does not include confusion. It does not include lies and deceit. It does not include accepting and taking on someone else's brokenness. And, it certainly does not include pouring all of yourself out, yet not having something of substance reciprocated. So, during the offseason — the time of preparation before engaging opportunities to connect and establish or strengthen relationships — recondition and do the work so that you can have a winning streak of wholeness. Also, be mindful in this recalibration and reconditioning that you do not revert back to old unhealthy habits, but continuously do your work to maintain your emotional makeover.

## The Never-Ending Mile: Maintaining Your Wholeness

When you are traveling on a long journey or any journey it is important for you to have certain tools in your car in case of an emergency. You need things that will allow you to continue your journey without having to completely stop because of a breakdown. Some of these items may include a tire pressure gauge, spare tire, tire wrench and jack, some emergency flares, jumper cables, a gas can and, depending on the conditions that in which you may be traveling, a snow brush, ice scraper, or shovel. In any case, you want to be prepared for your travels.

Tool 1: Accountability

One of the things that is a must-have tool on this journey is accountability... for every mile in this process. Without looking up the definition in a dictionary, if you break down the word accountability, it is the ability to account for something. So, having an accountability partner, better yet, several accountability partners and putting in accountability measures will ensure that you are not traveling on this journey alone, even if you are riding in the car alone. Having accountability partners does not necessarily mean that you are just telling your business to somebody, but accountability partners are people who can be trusted and who are going to cover you, counsel you, and check you to make sure that you stay on track to your process. Likewise, accountability partners are not people who are going to celebrate in your foolishness, but they are people who are going to make sure that in your brokenness those open areas will not be exposed but covered so that other things do not have a place to become lodged in to your soul. Accountability is necessary because, as one of my accountability partners said to me, the enemy of our soul thrives in lies and secrets. So, if the enemy wants an open door to get in and to wreak havoc in your life, he will do it through the things you keep a secret and are not honest with yourself about. Also, these accountability partners should be someone who is not necessarily having the same struggle but someone like a life coach, mentor, or counselor who has overcome in those areas and can give you strategy for how to continue on your journey.

Tool 2: Employ Discipline & Avoid Compromise

Likewise, wholeness requires discipline, and that discipline is necessary for you to avoid compromise. Discipline is a vital component for successfully remaining in wholeness. You must continue doing what you did to obtain your healing to maintain your healing. Consider the athlete who trains and practices in the off season. He must continue in order to maintain his stamina, endurance, agility, and prowess for competition. Another example is someone who is striving for weight loss and healthy living. If clean eating and exercise is what causes the desired physical transformation, then it will require that same discipline to keep it. And, when that person allows too many opportunities for "cheat days" (or compromise), the struggle intensifies to eliminate the appetite for unhealthy foods and habits that defeat the goal. In an honest reflection of my past, almost every area of struggle in my life was coupled with a place of compromise. I remember times when valuing my personal standard was a priority, and I did what was necessary to maintain right living. I also remember moments when I relaxed on my standards and compromised my wholeness trying to accommodate someone else brokenness. My life went from consecrated to compromising. I am not saying that you have to live life perfectly and that you won't make mistakes, but there is a difference between mistakes and bad decisions, flaws versus broken pieces, and discretion and privacy versus secrecy and lack of accountability. When you compromise you usually end up accepting someone else's compromise in their life. See, broken pieces plus broken pieces only equals more broken pieces. Your brokenness usually derives from a void somewhere in your life, and in trying to fill it, you compromise the authentic for something that is ingenuine or subpar. However, you must evaluate and ask yourself, "Why is it OK for me to accept someone else's broken pieces and compromise?" When I asked myself this question, my conclusion was that there was something within me that needed to be whole. I had to also be honest with what compromise looked like in my life in order to avoid it. For some, compromise looks like accepting the wrong type of attention from married people. It can look like being okay with having a secret and sexual relationship — good enough to bed but not good enough to wed. Sometimes compromise looks like flirting with any type of addiction. One of the most important factors in maintaining your healing and wholeness and avoiding compromise is knowing yourself, knowing your triggers, and knowing elements of your cycle so that you don't remain in or create a new cycle of bondage in your life. I am a firm believer that it is crucial to be careful of the triggers that undermine healing and wholeness because on this journey there is no room – ABSOLUTELY NO ROOM for compromise.

Tool 3: Use Your Voice

Another tool is the power of declaration. I heard Bishop T.D. Jakes preach a sermon referencing the woman with the issue of blood. The woman's healing was attached to her declaration that if she could just touch the hem of Jesus' garment she would be made whole. Bishop Jakes summed it powerfully stating, "What you say determines how far you go!" That notion is important on this journey. Proverbs 18: 21 says, "Death and life are in the power of the tongue." Death is indicated first in that scripture, which leads me to believe that it is our first inclination when making proclamations concerning our lives. We are so prone to speaking negativity into our lives (and lies into our soul) that we believe the horror story that our past experiences deemed would be our future. When we learn to speak life first and always — even before we actually feel or see it — the darkness of our reality is shined out by the light of the place of wholeness where we desire to live. Likewise, before we begin to speak and declare wholeness into our lives, it must start in our minds. Proverbs 23:7 affirms, "As a man thinks...so is he." Therefore, your healing begins in your mind. The mind equals our reasoning, logic, judgment, perception, and way of seeing things. We must renew our minds daily to remain healed, and understand that to become and remain healed and whole relies on the power of the scriptures and the power of our words. The word of God gives us strength and power over our mental and emotional well-being. We no longer have excuses to remain broken. No more pity party...only speak the promises of God.

## My Road Trip Called Life

As I reflect on each one of these miles, I think about how I have had to get off on an exit, reroute, and redo some of these miles over again. While, writing this book I was contemplating on how to share, how much to share, and what to share about my testimony, because even as I wrote this book, there was still pain from certain experiences and connections of which God was still healing and delivering me. I wanted to be able to share my story from a place of victory and overcoming and not a place of victimization and overwhelm though. Likewise, I wanted the narration of my truth to be as organic as possible. I guess the beginning of my relational scope is a good place to start.

Growing up in a household where there was a lot of love, care, and affection, I have always been one to build relationships early on as a child and through my adulthood. Sometimes that gift of relationship building has backfired because I was in a vulnerable place to be hurt, and because I moved out of the feelings and emotions in my heart without consulting the intelligence and strategy of my head. My experience with what I believed was love started in my adolescence and blossomed even more in high school. I got married at a young age, in my early 20s, and not to say that my age had anything to do with why my marriage did not last, but it had everything to do with recognizing that entering a covenant requires the two people entering into it to have the same level of emotional maturity to truly handle the responsibility that type of commitment demands. Getting married as college students, we were in the prime of still discovering who we were individually, and still maturing into adulthood. We fell in lust and in love, but as we grew further along in our situation, marriage became our solution to a values issue or a violation of our values as to how we were both raised. So instead of continuing to "shack up", we got married. In hindsight, I can admit that I was not spiritually mature enough to decipher the will of God for my life then, but in trying to do what was "right", I made a lifelong commitment into something that was not the right decision to make at that time.

Likewise, growing up, I have always been the honor student, the good girl, the church girl, the one who was accomplished and "on top" in everything I did, but even under all of that manmade perfection and my trying to live up to standards and wear the mask people placed upon me, something on the inside of me was broken, devoid, and unfulfilled. It is one thing for others to place a demand on the greatness inside of me, but my reality was that I constantly found myself trying to prove my worth to people instead of being who God created and called me to be, uniquely. I felt trapped in the box of people's perceptions and idea of me, my worth, and my value that I became absorbed in trying to live up to their standards instead of living abundantly (or as the song says, "my best life") in the wholeness of God's best intended for me.

I have experienced a failed marriage, dead-end relationships, an abortion, adultery, "shacking up", and having a child out of wedlock with broken promises of marriage. I have endured betrayal and even been the betrayer. I tend to love too hard, love too fast, and love too long. I have been in relationships where I was blinded to or accepted behaviors that, had I paid attention more closely and not been passive in expecting a reciprocation of "love" that was really nonexistent, I could have prevented the damage to my heart. Equally, I have fallen in love with men who were not honest about who they were and their true intentions. I have been played, used, emotionally abused, and endured embarrassment, hurt, rejection and abandonment as a result of me not truly knowing myself and valuing myself on a level that demanded what my heart desired.

While sometimes I wish that I could go back in time and rewrite my history, I stand in the peace and freedom to share the story of my journey. I had to get over my fear of what people would think in knowing my truth because I know the truth of my journey will empower others through their healing process. And, even though I provide this insight on how to navigate on this journey of wholeness, there are moments that I'm still living it and riding these same miles, just in a different place in my life. And, this time I am taking directions from the Passenger who has been here with me throughout the entire journey (Jesus)!

Sometimes, it is still difficult to own the entirety of my personal *Heal My Broken Pieces* experiences and reverting to my old ways of trying to appease the public court of opinion almost caused me not to publish this book. But, as one of my mentors encouraged me, "In your transparency, there is strength, and you are helping someone who may not be as strong as you to share their struggle." What I have come to realize is that in anything that I do I give my all; I pour all of myself into it. So, when

I moved from relationship to relationship not being totally healed, all of the broken pieces, fragments, and shards of myself left from my last, I poured into my next, and because I was not whole, I did not possess the capacity to be poured back into as I desired. Like me, so many people have carried broken pieces into a blessing (in the form of a relationship, friendship, networking connection, job opportunity or business venture) and tarnished the experience. As I stated at the beginning of this book, my desire is that after reading this book you will grow from brokenness to a perpetual place of inner healing and wholeness, filled with an abundance of contentment, joy, peace, and richness in your life and your relationships with others. I encourage you to continue to lean into your faith and into God through prayer, worship, and journaling, but also, I encourage you to seek professional counseling and intervention. It does not matter how long you have lived in the place of being broken, you have the power to choose and dwell in healing and wholeness…one mile at a time.

Peace and blessings to you in your personal *Heal My Broken Pieces* experience.

## Daily Affirmations

**Monday:** I transition from provision to promise; therefore, the cycle of brokenness is broken in my life.

**Tuesday:** There is nothing missing and nothing lacking in my life. I am empowered and equipped with all I need to move on from my past.

**Wednesday:** I am no longer bound to my brokenness; I am free in Christ.

**Thursday:** I will not return to the prison of brokenness from where my healing liberated me.

**Friday:** There are no more breeches and no more abortions to my destiny. I am whole so I can serve my life's purpose wholly.

**Saturday:** I am valuable and worthy of honor, respect, trust, and love.

**Sunday:** I am healed and whole; and will therefore maintain functional, holistic, and productive relationships and connections.

## Inner Healing & Emotional Wholeness Prayer

God, you are my creator and the lover of my soul. You know me better than I know myself. I sincerely ask You to heal my broken pieces. Divinely touch every broken area in my life. Change the narrative of my past and set me on a trajectory of triumph in overcoming all that I have experienced in life. Restore every broken expectation, mindset, and perception that I have of myself and others so that I can experience functional relationships, whether it is romantic, platonic, or filial. Empower me to employ the insight and strategies given to me and make me whole so that we can be my best self for myself, for others, and most importantly, for You. Lord, heal up and seal up every breach within my soul. Uproot every lie that has been planted in my heart and mind through words, dysfunction, and past trauma; and, deposit Your love, joy, and value inside so that I can begin to flourish and yield the fruit of healing and wholeness. Let Your strength be my portion and guide me in my interactions and connections. Shield me from anything that will cause emotional harm or setbacks. Grant me the wisdom, knowledge, understanding, and the power and willingness to do the work to experience the abundance of inner healing wholeness that Your love, peace, and grace offer. In the name of Jesus Christ, Amen!

## Emotional Healing Scriptures

Jeremiah 29:11 (KJV) - For I know the thoughts that I think toward you, saith the LORD, thoughts of peace, and not of evil, to give you an expected end.

Isaiah 43:2 (NLT) - When you go through deep waters, I will be with you. When you go through rivers of difficulty, you will not drown. When you walk through the fire of oppression, you will not be burned up; the flames will not consume you.

Psalm 34:17-18 (NLT) - The LORD hears his people when they call to him for help. He rescues them from all their troubles. The LORD is close to the brokenhearted; he rescues those whose spirits are crushed.

Psalm 147:3 (NIV) - He heals the brokenhearted and binds up their wounds.

1 Peter 5:7 (NLT) - Give all your worries and cares to God, for he cares about you

1 Peter 5:10 (NLT) - So after you have suffered a little while, he will restore, support, and strengthen you, and he will place you on a firm foundation.

Isaiah 53:5 (KJV) - But he was wounded for our transgressions, he was bruised for our iniquities: the chastisement of our peace was upon him; and with his stripes we are healed.

John 14:27 (AMP) - Do not let your heart be troubled, nor let it be afraid. [Let My perfect peace calm you in every circumstance and give you courage and strength for every challenge.]

Psalm 51:10 (KLV) - Create in me a clean heart, O God; and renew a right spirit within me.

2 Tim 1:7 (KJV) - For God hath not given us the spirit of fear; but of power, and of love, and of a sound mind.

Psalm 73:26 (AMP) - My flesh and my heart may fail, But God is the rock *and* strength of my heart and my portion forever.

Psalm 30:11(NLT) - You have turned my mourning into joyful dancing. You have taken away my clothes of mourning and clothed me with joy,

## About the Author

Author, TeShanna Rayner, is an educator, certified life coach, motivational speaker, and minister. She has a passion for equipping others with the knowledge, skills, and resources to push past any obstacle to better their lives and thrive in the abundance of wholeness. Using her expertise in Business and Education, along with her transformational coaching techniques and life experiences, she will continuously live out her purpose and passion to help others live an "Empowered Life Now!"

To book TeShanna Rayner as a speaker at your upcoming conference, event, panel, workshop or book club email empowercoacht@gmail.com.

For updates and information regarding coaching and consultation services please visit www.EmpoweredLifeNow.com.

www.ingramcontent.com/pod-product-compliance
Lightning Source LLC
LaVergne TN
LVHW041635070426
835507LV00008B/645